D1571282

Neopopulist Solutions to Neoliberal Problems

Mexico's National Solidarity Program

Denise Dresser

Printed with the assistance of the Tinker Foundation

Current Issue Brief No. 3
Center for U.S.-Mexican Studies
University of California, San Diego

1991

Printed in the United States of America by
the Center for U.S.-Mexican Studies
University of California, San Diego

ISBN 1-878367-06-4

Contents

Introduction

Mexico today is the country of "Solidarity." Solidarity slogans embellish town walls, Solidarity's accomplishments pervade the radio waves, and Mexican pop stars sing the Hymn of Solidarity. "Solidarity" is the popular reference to the Mexican government's National Solidarity Program (PRONASOL), an umbrella organization aimed at developing health, education, nutrition, housing, employment, infrastructure, and other productive projects to benefit the seventeen million Mexicans living in extreme poverty. Critics see PRONASOL as a social tranquilizer, the government's effort to redeem a population that its current economic policies further impoverish. Advocates, on the other hand, hail PRONASOL as a crucial complement to the country's economic restructuring program, a formula for linking democracy with social justice. Both groups agree that the program has become the Salinas administration's political trademark; PRONASOL is credited with helping propel the dominant Institutional Revolutionary Party (PRI) to a stunning victory in the 1991 midterm elections.

This essay analyzes PRONASOL as a political strategy and argues that deeper and broader purposes and implications underlie what government officials present as assistance to the poverty stricken. PRONASOL constitutes a core element in the Salinas administration's governability formula, and it illustrates the complex linkages between politics and policy in a context of economic adjustment. The government designed PRONASOL to meet three sets of objectives: (1) to adapt the state's traditional social role to new economic constraints and redefine the limits of its intervention in the context of a neoliberal reform strategy; (2) to diffuse potential social discontent through selective subsidies, accommodate social

This essay draws from Dresser n.d. Special thanks are due to Maria Cook, Diane Davis, Juan Enríquez, Jonathan Fox, Robin King, John Lear, Kevin Middlebrook, Juan Molinar, and John Sheahan for comments on an earlier draft.

mobilization through "co-participation," and undermine the strength of left-wing opposition forces by establishing ties with and commitments to popular movements; and (3) to restructure local and regional PRI elites under an increased degree of centralized control. In sum, by greasing the wheels of the neoliberal train and laying down the tracks that allow that train to move forward, PRONASOL aims to improve political sustainability.

The Salinas administration came to power in a context of deteriorating traditional forms of political control, divisions in the government elite, fractures within the one-party system, and weakened presidential authority. Mexico's 1988 presidential campaign and election attested to the PRI's declining electoral clout, the appeal of Cuauhtémoc Cárdenas and the left-wing FDN (National Democratic Front), and the durability of the conservative opposition PAN (National Action Party). With the legitimacy of Salinas's victory widely disputed, the PRI emerged from the election as a party ideologically out of touch with its electorate, poorly organized, badly led, and unable to win elections effectively. As a result, skeptics and optimists alike augured a major political realignment and a possible democratic transition—particularly after Salinas himself declared the end of the hegemonic party system.

Nevertheless, three years and many local elections later, sober skepticism has replaced the heady optimism of 1988. Promises of political reform have apparently given way to political consolidation, decentralization to centralized control, parliamentarism to renewed presidentialism, and the PRI's twilight to the (albeit questionable) party's electoral rebirth. Opposition political parties that seemed capable of propelling Mexico into the multiparty era now appear wracked by divergent tendencies struggling between compromise and confrontation, between rupture or engagement with the regime. Mexico's political involution since July 1988 conjures up images of Penelope's loom: what was woven during the day unraveled by night.

The politics of PRONASOL sheds light on why hegemonic parties like the PRI can survive even when threatened by powerful alternative organizations, and why the party has apparently been able to revive after a period of crisis and decline. PRONASOL is strengthening the party—particularly the pro-Salinas factions—by providing renewed sources of patronage. By channeling resources into the PRI, PRONASOL enhances the party's elasticity and staying power. PRONASOL is a containment strategy devised to provide the PRI with breathing space to reform itself marginally, while squeezing out the opposition.

PRONASOL is also key to understanding why the Salinas administration has been able to proceed full speed ahead with economic restructuring without engaging in substantial political reform. By providing welfare benefits in the form of a poverty alleviation program to disaffected popular groups, the administration has secured the support necessary to continue in a neoliberal direction while still controlling the most important decision areas. PRONASOL's selective rewards and concessions to popular sectors serve to strengthen the PRI's political cards and weaken those of the opposition.

However, the main criticism of PRONASOL is not its use as an instrument to solidify the grip of the PRI. Most democracies carry out social programs in exchange for political support. PRONASOL even deserves credit as a nonrepressive way of easing the underprivileged into the new economic system. What is particularly wrong with PRONASOL is that it builds upon and reinforces some basic flaws in the country's political system. PRONASOL is run out of the president's private pocket, its beneficiaries are selected on personalistic and partisan political grounds, and, most fundamentally, it is immune from any democratic means of control or accountability. As a result, PRONASOL may strengthen institutions and practices—such as presidentialism and unfair competition among parties—that constitute the main obstacles to political change in Mexico.

What follows is an initial approximation to the political aspects of PRONASOL. However, PRONASOL is an ongoing program; it continues to evolve and grow. As a result, many of its long-term consequences are still unclear. PRONASOL has awakened great expectations about improved living standards, popular involvement in decision making, and a truly participatory form of development. Whether or not PRONASOL will live up to those expectations and how it will influence the country's political scenario remain questions for the future.

Nuts and Bolts of the Program

A central theme of Salinas's presidential campaign was government concern for the poor. Recognizing that Mexico's severe economic crisis had taken its toll on large sectors of the population, Salinas promised assistance, drawing up a list of 2,115 commitments to popular groups, including pledges to build schools, support peasant agriculture, and provide potable water, paved streets, sewerage, and electricity. Once in office, Salinas established PRO-NASOL, which since December 1988 has directed a flow of public resources into housing, power generation, roads, and other forms of infrastructure. According to official figures, PRONASOL operated with a budget of U.S. $680 million in 1989, $950 million in 1990, and an estimated $1.7 billion in 1991—1.1, 1.5, and 2.2 percent, respectively, of total budgeted federal government spending during these three years (*Gaceta de Solidaridad* 25 [April 1991]: 25). The increasing visibility and scope of PRONASOL suggest that it operates with a much larger pool of resources than those presented in the public account. However, it is virtually impossible to gauge the extent of off-budget funds that PRONASOL receives from the sale of public enterprises and relabeled categories of social/infrastructure spending at the state and federal levels (see table 1).

Salinas's PRONASOL staff record the popular demands made of the president during his weekly tours of the countryside. Solidarity committees at the grassroots level then design projects, in collaboration with government staff, to address these demands.[1] Funds are subsequently disbursed to the committees to support public works or to complement regional development

---

[1] Solidarity committees mobilize and organize community members, evaluate proposed public works, and supervise their implementation. Approximately sixty-four thousand committees have been established over the last three years (Presidencia de la República Mexicana n.d.).

TABLE 1

COMPOSITION OF EXPENDITURES FOR SOCIAL DEVELOPMENT
(AS A PERCENTAGE OF TOTAL SPENDING)

	1988	1989	1990	1991
SOCIAL DEVELOPMENT	14.9	17.9	21.8	26.5
Education	6.4	7.6	8.9	11.0
Health and Labor	6.9	8.5	10.6	12.3
Solidarity and Regional Development	0.6	1.1	1.5	2.2
Urban Development	1.0	0.7	0.8	1.0

Source: *Agenda presupuestal 1991.* Mexico: Secretaría de Programación y Presupuesto, 1991, pp. 36 and 45.

programs in four strategic areas: food support, production, social services, and infrastructure.[2]

Food support is provided through general subsidies and targeted coverage for vulnerable groups, including the rural and urban poor. The total cost of these programs (including PRONASOL's contribution) was approximately U.S. $900 million in 1988 and $1,400 million in 1989.[3] Targeted coverage for the urban poor consists of subsidized tortillas and milk sold to families earning less than twice the minimum wage. In 1988 subsidized tortillas and milk were provided to approximately 1.08 and 1.86 million families, respectively, at an estimated cost of $195 million.

The government targets the rural poor through CONASUPO, its food marketing and distribution agency. CONASUPO stores sell basic staples at subsidized prices and in principle serve a covered population of 5.1 million families. The total estimated cost of the program in 1988 was $51 million. Between 1989 and 1990, PRONASOL increased the number of CONASUPO stores by 33 percent and milk plants by 66 percent. The government's Nutrition and Health Program also targets vulnerable groups, providing free food, health and nutrition information, and basic health coverage. In 1988, at a total cost of $1.7 million, this program helped 215,000 families living in acute poverty. Other programs supervised by the National System for the Integral Development of the Family (DIF) covered 1.1 million families in 1988, at a cost of $100 per family per year.

To supplement these broad government programs, PRONASOL established three programs aimed at increasing the potential

---

[2]Solidarity for Social Welfare includes measures related to health, education, food, housing, and urban services; Solidarity for Production focuses on measures that support agricultural activities, channeling of resources to campesinos and micro-industries. See Valdez 1990.

[3]Data are drawn from Levy 1991; Solís Cámara 1991.

earnings of the poor. Solidarity Funds for Production in 1990 provided credit to 400,000 farmers engaged in high-risk, low-yield activities and established collaborative agreements with 349 producer organizations. Solidarity Funds for Indigenous Communities channeled $20 million for 18,000 local development projects to fifty ethnic groups in diverse regions. Women in Solidarity has supported incorporating women into productive activities by providing credit to 151,000 women setting up small workshops and industries (*Gaceta de Solidaridad* 25 [April 15, 1991]: 17).

PRONASOL's social services programs seek to expand the country's health infrastructure and educational facilities. The Solidarity Health Program has established 758 new clinics (a 33 percent increase over the number of clinics existing in 1988), rehabilitated and expanded twenty-six hospitals, and incorporated 1.4 million people under its coverage. The Solidarity School Program has improved 34,000 schools, awarded 115,000 scholarships, and provided health and food support to schoolchildren and their families by providing food baskets. In total, more than four million primary and secondary schoolchildren have benefited from the program.

PRONASOL programs have also supported infrastructure development in poor communities through channels like the Municipal Solidarity Funds. During 1990 funds were distributed to meet "urgent investment needs" in 1,426 municipalities in thirteen states. According to PRONASOL officials, these programs have provided electricity to five million low-income homes, improved water supply to seven hundred urban communities, and built nine thousand kilometers of rural roads. In addition, PRONASOL has delivered 750,000 property titles to residents in urban squatter settlements.

PRONASOL rejects the broad system of subsidies and the high levels of social expenditures of the 1970s in favor of a more selective approach: in principle, for greater efficiency in targeting the poor; in practice, for adapting the state's traditional social role to the fiscal stringencies of a streamlined economy. The Salinas team has justified the shift from broad-based social expenditures to minimalist programs by arguing that the scarcity of resources forces public spending to be selective. Under Salinas we are witnessing a transition from ubiquitous state intervention to strategic, targeted, and compensatory intervention. In a context of scarce resources the political elite want to slim down the state *and* maximize the discretionary allocation of resources. PRONASOL marks the emergence of a new kind of "statism" that champions survival of the fittest in some sectors but allows "inefficient" groups—like the poor targeted by PRONASOL—to survive in others.

Under direct orders from the Office of the President, PRO-NASOL funds have been used to shift the scope and content of state intervention in the economy. Public allocations are moving to communications, energy, and social services at the municipal level and declining sharply in areas like manufacturing.[4] It seems that under Salinas Mexico City will see no ambitious industrialization projects, massive health programs, or spectacular public works. The Salinas team appears to be following Michel Crozier's dictum, "Modern state, modest state." Salinas supports this shift by arguing that the government must regain its capacity to address social demands. Public resources are to "provide small solutions to big problems" (García Soler 1989).

Implicit in this argument is a reformulation of a key goal traditionally associated with the Mexican postrevolutionary state: the promotion of social justice. All modern Mexican presidents have felt compelled to demonstrate that their programs promoted development and social justice; Salinas is no exception. But PRO-NASOL departs in important ways from the programs espoused by Salinas's predecessors. Before Salinas, social justice meant government support for organized labor and ejido agriculture through broad-based subsidies, wage increases, and agrarian reform. PRONASOL's strategies are less class based, corporatist, and distributive, and more politically selective and targeted. The underlying assumption is that selective state support will be more politically efficient than generalized subsidies; i.e., PRONASOL may provide more political bang for the buck. Officially, however, PRONASOL is not a break from the state's revolutionary commitments, but rather the only program able to reestablish the state's true social role, which had been undermined by populist squandering over many administrations.

In emphasizing the role of societal groups in alleviating poverty, PRONASOL marks a shift from the state as benefactor to the state as partner in development. The Salinas administration has widely publicized its new form of state-society relations based on:

> joining the cause of others, participating in actions
> that benefit others, organizing and managing re-
> sources carefully. It is a form of relating with
> society that has always characterized campesinos

---

[4]Grupo de Economistas y Asociados (GEA) indicates that public investment is channeled increasingly into basic social and urban services through PRONASOL and estimates that 50 percent of public investment in 1990 was carried out through PRONASOL programs. GEA warns, however, that "although public investment has increased in social welfare areas, there are no spending figures available that allow [us] to determine its exact amount and destination, therefore limiting the analysis" (GEA 1991: 23).

> and workers, Indian communities, and families.
> The government of Mexico recognizes the value of
> solidarity in the fight against extreme poverty
> (Presidencia de la República Mexicana n.d.: 1).

PRONASOL encourages program beneficiaries to participate in defining program priorities and to co-finance projects with their own resources. In principle, implementation and decision making result from the combined efforts of government and program participants. Through its emphasis on co-responsibility, the program is entrusting the allocation of scarce resources to the organized beneficiaries themselves and encouraging their participation in policy decisions. Instead of establishing top-down bureaucratic structures, the program aims to build on representative local organizations in both urban and rural areas. This emphasis on community participation can be explained in part by the government's drive to enhance PRONASOL's accountability and effectiveness. However, popular participation in solving community problems also functions to generate political support for government-sponsored development programs, and consequently for the political system itself (see Salinas de Gortari 1984).

PRONASOL authorities contend that the program differs from its antecedents because it builds on identifying natural representatives at the community level and then coordinating municipal, state, and federal actors in bringing projects to fruition. For example, Undersecretary of Planning and Budget Carlos Rojas has argued that popular participation such as the provision of manual labor can protect against paternalism, bureaucratization, and corruption (Rojas 1990).

Government officials have gone to great lengths to present PRONASOL as a government program, as opposed to an instrument of the PRI. Salinas has declared on numerous occasions that PRONASOL is open to all. Program authorities stress that PRONASOL's search for grassroots actors willing to assume co-responsibility has not been exclusionary and that many independent organizations as well as groups linked to opposition parties have participated in solidarity committees and accords. PRONASOL claimed in early 1991 to be operating in 171 out of 173 municipalities controlled by the opposition (personal interview, Mexico City, March 1991).

PRONASOL authorities have also used the notion of co-participation to deflect criticism about the increasingly evident populist tendencies and political objectives of the program. According to PRONASOL spokesmen, the program is not populist since it is based on real resources, not the government's ability to print currency. Salinas's promises need public participation to become realities; people, not bureaucracies, define the goals. As Olga Elena Peña Martínez observed, "'populism' means to offer without really intending to deliver. PRONASOL breaks with that idea because government commitments are based on the decisions of the community about what it needs. Salinas's efforts are popular, not populist, because citizens participate in constructing public works, supervise their execution, and assure transparency in the use of resources" (Macías García 1991). PRONASOL's ideological underpinnings are based on the Salinas definition of populism as an irrational set of self-destructive economic measures to redistribute income through deficit spending. Mexican state elites condemn populism as an economic and political mistake. They argue that PRONASOL does not jeopardize the state's fiscal health, nor does it engage in political manipulation. PRONASOL is not populist because its resources are limited and its beneficiaries define their needs instead of submitting to government mandates.

A Preliminary Assessment

Even a preliminary evaluation of PRONASOL is difficult; many of its subprograms are still being implemented and relevant data regarding their impact on the population are not yet available. Nevertheless, an assessment of the program in its current shape and form indicates that PRONASOL is little more than a short-term, compensatory program with partial and selective economic impact. The targeted food programs exemplify this focus as they transfer purchasing power primarily to the urban poor. In addition to this bias against the rural poor, it is not even clear whether PRONASOL's food support resources channeled into the rural areas reach the very poor. Of a total of U.S. $900 million spent in 1988 on food and health support by PRONASOL programs, only about $500 million benefited the most impoverished.[5]

PRONASOL guidelines restrict municipal funds investments to no more than fifty million pesos (U.S. $17,000) per project, and this limitation precludes community projects that go beyond simple remedies or secondary repairs. Not only are current PRONASOL expenditures only partially effective, but, given the extent of poverty in Mexico, the 1 or 1.5 percent of GNP invested in PRONASOL is insufficient. PRONASOL's 1991 entitlements represent approximately one-tenth of the outlays devoted to interest payments on Mexico's foreign debt.[6] If we were to divide PRONASOL's budget for 1990 by the seventeen million people in Mexico who live in extreme poverty, each would have received a daily allotment of 15 cents.

---

[5]Santiago Levy argues that in order for the income transfers through food support programs to be truly effective, information and services related to fertility control, food conservation, and basic health care would need to be strengthened. PRONASOL has yet to address these loopholes. See Levy 1991: 77–78.

[6]Approximately U.S. $20 billion will be disbursed for debt interest payments, compared to $1.7 billion allotted to PRONASOL. See El Mercado de Valores 24 (December 15, 1990): 7.

PRONASOL's efforts to channel more resources to the poor are a welcome development, particularly in light of the spending limits imposed by the Salinas administration's macroeconomic stabilization program. However, the success of poverty alleviation programs is not determined by their level of resource allocation but by their capacity to address the roots of poverty. The structural causes of poverty lie in the concentration of asset ownership (primarily capital), population pressures that hold down the value of labor relative to property, regressive taxation, and unequal access to educational opportunities, skill acquisition, and health care. A frontal attack on poverty must incorporate policies that contribute to a better distribution of productive assets and income. Such policies include giving high priority to social spending in federal and state budgets, establishing selective subsidies to support productive activities, adopting price stabilization policies, and promoting monetary and credit policies that perceive social welfare as part of the country's development strategy (see CCPNS 1990). The government has adopted some of these policies over the last few years in an effort to redirect market outcomes to benefit the poor. But unless further reforms address the primary determinants of poverty, PRONASOL's activities will be overwhelmed by the tide.

PRONASOL's critics have called for a more integral pro-poor approach to the design of the adjustment measures themselves.[7] Such an approach should be applied, they argue, at every level of adjustment choices: in the mix and phasing of macroeconomic measures, and in the priorities and design of sectoral policies and specific programs and projects. Poverty alleviation efforts, they contend, should focus on the allocation of costs in social expenditures and subsidies, as well as on wage policies. The call for redesigning macroeconomic packages—such as infrastructure development, credit programs, and pricing policies—to spare the poor has had little impact among economic planners in Mexico. The overall severity of the austerity measures adopted, the depth of cuts in government expenditures and subsidies, and current wage policies indicate that efficiency concerns continue to outweigh equity concerns.

During his second State of the Union address, Salinas indicated that the wage restraints of the Pact for Stability and Economic Growth (PECE) would remain in place, arguing that the real value of the minimum wage could recover only if inflation were held under control. The sixth phase of the PECE coincided with contin-

---

[7]For a sampling of criticisms made of PRONASOL see Aziz Nassif 1990; Rascón 1990; Moguel 1990.

ued low levels of social spending accompanied by renewed price hikes in public services.[8] In Mexico City alone, the price of all public services increased by 20 percent, and differential rate increases for water and property taxes measured 20–319 percent and 33–1241 percent respectively (Acosta and Galarza 1989: 13). In 1990–91, CONASUPO, the state food distributor, trimmed its operations by closing stores, eliminating subsidies, and selling off subsidiary companies. According to its director, Ignacio Ovalle, the purpose was to reduce CONASUPO benefits to the rich and increase benefits to the poor. Overall subsidies decreased by 66.4 percent in real terms between 1989 and 1990 (GEA 1991: 23).

This emphasis on efficiency might seem a logical counterpart of decisions to allow real minimum wages to fall. Support for minimum wages straddles a crucial dividing line between concerns for economic efficiency and concerns for equitable income distribution. In Mexico's case, as in most others, the balance of public choice moves between the efficiency side and the distribution side. The stress on liberalization since 1985 seems to have pushed the balance in Mexico further toward efficiency considerations than ever before, at the expense of employment and real incomes for those at the lowest wage levels.[9]

PRONASOL authorities have incorporated some suggestions made by their council of policy analysts and academics—the need for a "basic social floor" and the notion of "neediest groups"—but PRONASOL has yet to implement measures that would lead to participatory development. As Enrique González Tiburcio, a member of the council, argued:

> Until now, PRONASOL has depended on residual public spending, but it cannot forever be subjected to the ebbs and flows of Mexico's macroeconomic policy. PRONASOL has been nurtured by finite funds like those derived from the sale of public-sector enterprises. One of the program's most important challenges is of a financial nature. A supposedly long-term social program cannot depend on extraordinary budget flows. It must

---

[8] In 1990 social expenditure as a percentage of total expenditure amounted to 28.8 percent, 10 percentage points below its level in 1980. See IMF 1991.

[9] If anything, current macroeconomic policies in Mexico (like free trade, further elimination of controls and subsidies, and increasing reliance on private markets) seem to be leaning toward measures that are unlikely to favor participatory development. For further elaboration of this argument see Sheahan 1991. Sheahan finds that Mexican real wages in the 1980s declined more sharply than wages in other Latin American countries. As late as 1989, wage payments as a percentage of GDP amounted to only 23.1 percent, compared to 37.5 percent in 1981.

have a structural and permanent link (personal
interview, Mexico City, March 19, 1991).

The goal of most social programs is to raise living standards,
an objective usually accomplished through income-generating
strategies, employment-generating strategies, and social spending. PRONASOL acts as a vehicle for allocating social spending that
might lead to the emergence of a basic social floor, particularly
regarding infrastructure. It would, however, have a more redistributive impact if macroeconomic policies simultaneously gener-
ated employment and elevated incomes (Provencio 1990). One
expert on poverty alleviation programs noted: "If GNP grows at 3.5
percent annually, all other things equal, it would take sixty years to
eradicate poverty" (Warman interview, *Proceso*, March 27, 1988).

Populism Revisited

Much of PRONASOL is not new; many of the program's strategies are streamlined versions of old populist formulas. Traditional populist policies implemented by previous administrations included state planning, employment, and welfare programs that frequently advocated popular involvement. Both the Caminos de Mano de Obra program under Luis Echeverría (1970–76) and COPLAMAR, enacted by Miguel de la Madrid (1982–88), emphasized the organized inclusion of popular communities (through the provision of manual labor) into state-sponsored development programs.[10] The recurrence of such populist programs in Mexico responds to a time-honored political logic: the need to incorporate emergent or dissatisfied groups into national politics.

The main difference between previous programs and PRONASOL is the latter's explicit goal of capturing support for the PRI in a context of increased party competitiveness. Jonathan Fox noted that in the case of CONASUPO-COPLAMAR, reformist policy makers were willing to take the risks inherent in promoting genuine community participation in order to offset the power of local elites, even if that participation did not automatically translate into support for the PRI (Fox 1991). PRONASOL came into being in a much different political context in which the active presence and mobilizing capacity of the left-wing Party of the Democratic Revolution (PRD) had raised the political stakes. As a result, PRONASOL officials opted for selective compensation and targeting formulas in order to guide grassroots collective action

[10]Under the Caminos de Mano de Obra program, the federal government provided materials and technical assistance for the construction of dirt roads in remote rural areas; the individual communities involved provided the necessary labor. In 1979 the Mexican government established a national community-managed rural food distribution program (CONASUPO-COPLAMAR) that created a national network of thousands of community stores supplying subsidized food to Mexico's lowest-income population. See Fox 1986.

into partisan political affiliation, or at least out of the folds of the opposition.

In the initial stages of economic stabilization and adjustment under de la Madrid, the Mexican government's shrinking resource base precluded it from compensating key constituencies through public spending, and between 1982 and 1988 practically all government social programs were either eliminated or greatly reduced. The populace responded with the electoral upheaval of 1988. Hoping to win back the PRI's lost bases of support, the Salinas team included pro-poor measures in its restructuring agenda, namely, channeling public resources to select groups through PRONASOL.

PRONASOL's initiatives build on the enduring appeal of populist rhetoric. Echoes of populism reverberate in the government's campaign to promote PRONASOL because the program—like its predecessors—pursues a key goal on the populist agenda: building constituencies among the urban and rural underprivileged. PRONASOL's pivotal departure from previous programs is that along with its social welfare message, it explicitly endorses economic liberalization. Populist policies traditionally rallied political coalitions in favor of import-substituting industrialization, but now they serve to gather support for free-market economic measures. For example, Salinas justified divestment of the state airline, Mexicana de Aviación, by arguing that continued public ownership would consume resources that otherwise would be used to assist the poor. During his 1990 European tour, Salinas indicated that income from that sale provided electricity to 500,000 residents of one of Mexico's poorest regions. By associating it with redistribution, Mexico's leaders are recasting a generally unpalatable privatization drive as prerequisite to gaining social justice for the country's lower-income strata.

Even though privatization has little to offer the very poor beyond the unverifiable channeling of finite resources to PRONASOL, the perception that resources derived from the sale of inefficient state firms are used to provide social benefits does allow state elites to intensify public-sector reform. The links between privatization and PRONASOL permit the Salinas team to declare that social considerations are guiding the dismantling of the state and leading to a new, socially determined form of state intervention in the economy (Loaeza 1989). By combining the efficiency objective of privatization with the social welfare objectives of PRONASOL, Salinas hopes to institutionalize a streamlined state that can continue to intervene on a compensatory and discretionary basis. The difficulty in tracing the source and amount of PRONASOL's resources, largely under the control of the Office of the President and the Ministry of Planning and Budget, suggests the discretionary and highly politicized orientation of its programs. Executive groups directly under presidential supervision coordinate and centralize the work (and funds) of existing social welfare institutions to suit PRONASOL's purposes. This parallel institutional network enables Salinas to use vast resources and carry our significant programs without congressional scrutiny or the pressures of party politics. Thus resources from the president's private pocket can be targeted strategically according to electoral calendars and specific political needs.

At the same time, the administration repeatedly emphasizes PRONASOL's limited budget as part of a deliberate strategy attesting to the diminished role of the state and the transparency of public resource allocation. PRONASOL has not been presented as a long-term, large, and income-producing resource transfer from privileged groups. The time horizons of PRONASOL programs in all likelihood will not exceed Salinas's term in office, and, at least officially, state authorities portray the resource transfers involved as meager. Not coincidentally, among members of the Mexican private sector and World Bank and international financial circles, compensatory programs are viewed as the least politically controversial category of pro-poor action, precisely because of their perceived short-term, urgent, and charitable nature and their emphasis on targeted versus generalized subsidies.

Following World Bank guidelines, PRONASOL combines targeting with a sense of urgency. As Salinas argued: "We cannot wait until economic recovery begins to make decisions that support the welfare of Mexicans who have less" (Salinas de Gortari 1988: 5). Early evaluations of PRONASOL reveal, however, that the program may not be focusing sufficiently on the neediest—particularly those in rural areas—mainly because of political objectives unrelated to poverty alleviation.

Allowing political considerations to force PRONASOL into a vast array of areas and projects will probably dilute the program's impact. As the following section suggests, targeting strategies are being shaped by political concerns as well as by socioeconomic and "marginality" indicators. The political linkages between PRONASOL and partisan concerns are particularly evident in the *tortivale* program.[11] Its coverage has been directed mainly toward urban areas—particularly the Federal District, including Mexico City—where the PRI suffered heavy losses in the 1988 presidential election. PRONASOL's effectiveness as a poverty alleviation program thus is being limited not only by macroeconomic constraints

---

[11] *Tortivales* (coupons for one free kilo of tortillas per day) were established to substitute for the 50 percent reduction in subsidies for tortillas announced in July 1990.

but also by political imperatives. PRONASOL is more than an economic buffer to soften the effects of adjustment on vulnerable groups; it is also a weapon against the opposition and a political tool to link public and popular organizations and thus resolve Mexico's problems of political representation. PRONASOL may have been an economic afterthought to offset certain effects of the country's restructuring strategy, but it has become part of a broader political logic promoted by state elites: maintaining political support through state patronage. This dual orientation generates further problems. Insofar as PRONASOL ceases to be a program with clearly limited plans and resources and becomes the president's personal fund for political crusades, the program loses sight of the reforms required to address the roots of poverty.

Stealing the Enemy's Thunder

The strategy and impact of PRONASOL policies reveal a partisan political agenda that includes establishing ties to autonomous popular movements, designing new forms of linkage between state and society, building a constituency for a restructured PRI, and realigning local and regional party elites. As a strategy of governance PRONASOL's fundamental objective is to lay the ground rules for renewed clientelist policies at all levels of government, and especially with popular sectors sympathetic to the left-wing Party of the Democratic Revolution.

Insofar as popular movements do not represent the birth of civil society as much as the creation of political subjects within civil society, PRONASOL can—by addressing the material needs and demands for participation that propelled the movements into the political arena—deactivate them. The roots of the *neocardenista* movement have been shriveling of their own accord but also as a result of deliberate state action. Through the selective distribution of material rewards, state leaders intend to mobilize popular groups in support of the regime–to win popular sympathies, or at least curb antipathies that could translate into electoral gains for the opposition.

PRONASOL's "divide, buy off, and conquer" strategies have proved highly successful among Mexico's disparate popular movements. Historically these movements have been divided by differences in goals, tactics, and leadership. In a paradoxical twist, political participation, through the *neocardenista* National Democratic Front and later the Party of the Democratic Revolution, that spurred the growth of popular movements has also created conditions for internal competition and division. A key problem is that in its transition from a social movement to a political party, *neocardenismo* has been plagued by seemingly inevitable problems of bureaucratization and political infighting. Elections for the PRD

National Council in 1990, for example, revealed rancorous disputes along complex intergroup and interparty lines. In light of increasing political battles within the PRD, analysts may be correct in pointing out that it is giving priority to the logic of power over the social logic that led to its creation. To the extent that PRD politicians use popular movements to strengthen their leverage in power struggles within the party, they tend to neglect their constituencies. Issues of central concern for popular movements—sectoral and regional autonomy, independence, pluralism, respect for the right to establish political alliances, and the possibility for broad representation—have often been pushed to the back burner, opening a window of opportunity for the government acting through PRONASOL.

Even though *neocardenismo* stands out as an unusually successful social movement, its concrete victories as a political party have been limited and partial, especially given its tremendous efforts to mobilize the population. Its numerous defeats in the 1989 and 1990 local elections and its difficulty in winning relatively minor victories have reduced its ranks. Some organizations affiliated to the FDN in 1988 have dropped out of the alliance, underscoring the fragility of *neocardenismo's* political face. Doubts are surfacing whether support for Cárdenas can be translated effectively into support for the PRD.

PRONASOL's strategies have built upon and contributed to the growing detachment between popular movements and political causes and parties. PRONASOL has capitalized on the opposition's incapacity to improve living conditions substantially for large sectors of the Mexican people. Although leaders of popular movements in Mexico may still be interested in broader political issues— such as democratization—many grassroots participants are moved to political action by the prospect of material benefits for their neighborhoods. The logic behind PRONASOL's activities in selected areas is that the program addresses the core needs of the population in a way that the opposition cannot. Program officials present new services as a gift from the state, even when they respond directly to demands posed earlier by PRD activists.

Another hurdle for the opposition is the fact that even among the poor there are conflicting material interests and priorities: land titles for some, water and electricity for others, etc. PRONASOL's selective use of resources intensifies this preexisting segmentation, since a minor victory for one neighborhood may mean a major loss for another. The selective distribution of tortillas through the *tortivale* program to urban popular groups, for example, has caused resentment among campesinos who feel that the state is neglecting them. A leader of the Independent Confederation of

Agricultural Workers and Peasants (CIOAC) lamented: "Now it turns out the Indians are less needy than the workers" (personal interview, Mexico City, March 19, 1991).

This competition over scarce resources undermines the cross-sectoral and cross-regional front that popular movements established in 1988 and cuts to the core of their political performance. *Neocardenismo* reversed the tendency of popular movements to sectorialize their demands, instead inserting them into a broad national project under the aegis of charismatic leadership. In Cuauhtémoc Cárdenas, popular movements found a point of consensus around which to organize, generalize their demands, and politicize their struggles. Labor leaders, urban groups, peasants, and Indians converged in their support for Cárdenas, temporarily forgetting their sectoral struggles. PRONASOL, in contrast, underscores particularistic affiliations and goals through the specificity of its programs and regional targeting strategies.

PRONASOL's co-participation strategies reflect the Salinas government's emphasis on concertation with independent, non-PRI groups. During his tenure as secretary of planning and budget, Salinas already showed an interest in promoting concertation with autonomous organizations (Harvey 1990). Then after the electoral watershed of 1988, his administration moved to negotiate a new relationship between the state and popular movements, apparently bowing to the inevitable. By providing financial and technical assistance through concertation accords, PRONASOL has managed to identify itself with the democratic social sector of self-managed rural enterprises and autonomous popular-movement coordinating committees.

For example, PRONASOL has established working relationships with campesino organizations affiliated to the National Union of Regional Peasant Organizations (UNORCA) through Solidarity Funds for Production and the Nueva Laguna Program (*El Nacional* 1991). The Democratic Peasant Front of Chihuahua, the Independent Federation of Agricultural Workers and Peasants (FIOAC), the National "Plan de Ayala" Coordinating Committee (CNPA), and certain factions of the National Coordinating Committee of the Urban Popular Movement (CONAMUP) have also joined the ranks of PRONASOL's beneficiaries. However, the coordination and collaboration promoted by PRONASOL strategists is proving to be a double-edged sword, able to undermine not only the autonomy of popular organizations but also their internal cohesion. Organizations that engage in concertation are not monolithic entities; their leaders hold varying perceptions of the risks involved in such negotiating. What is viewed as a loss of autonomy by some leaders may be interpreted as pragmatic political compromise and tactical alliance building by others. In October 1990, for example, important factions within UNORCA led a major protest march against the Salinas administration; others among its leadership, more sympathetic to the regime, had already joined the government in negotiations.

PRONASOL may be dividing popular movements and taking the anti-government steam out of independent groups, but the degree to which it undermines their autonomy remains unclear. Co-participation allows popular organizations to retain at least formal independence and to feel that they have willingly entered into alliance with the state. PRONASOL thus goes beyond traditional strategies of co-optation, which involve more obvious political subordination through external intervention in internal decision-making processes. But no matter how much PRONASOL officials emphasize the program's respect for the autonomy of popular movements, the fact remains that PRONASOL ties them to the state's distributional network, and consequently may render them vulnerable to government demands for political loyalty.

The case of the Committee for Popular Defense (CDP) in the state of Durango is a telling example of PRONASOL's impact on popular movements (see Haber 1989; Moguel 1991). Since the mid-1980s the CDP has proved adept at carrying out public works, mobilizing the population, presenting forceful demands to the state government, and developing a regional political presence through legislative office. Like most popular organizations, the CDP was responsive to PRONASOL overtures, for two reasons. First, the CDP was competing directly with official organizations to provide material benefits to its constituents, and its survival depended on its ability to deliver. Second, the CDP had grown increasingly dissatisfied with the PRD's lack of responsiveness to popular movement concerns and with the unclear policy alternatives of the Cárdenas coalition. In early 1989 the CDP decided to enter independently into an accord with PRONASOL whereby federal, state, municipal, and CDP resources were combined to support public works projects and CDP-owned and operated businesses. Salinas gained politically from signing the accord, dividing the left and diluting opposition to the regime in the region. After signing the agreement, the CDP broke with the PRD and abstained from criticizing Salinas and his policies. Political acquiescence toward the government appears to have been part of the bargain for receiving PRONASOL benefits, and the CDP complied.

Subsequently the CDP joined other key PRONASOL partners to form a new national political party of the "social left," the Labor Party (PT), referred to by some critics as the "PRONASOL Party." The PT has provided groups like the CDP with a national political option while permitting them to retain access to government social programs. The question is whether that access will condition the political future of the PT and transform it into a parastatal party contrived to lure away important segments of the PRD's constituency.

Reversing the 1988 electoral victories of the PRD appears to be a significant part of PRONASOL's political agenda. Very early on, PRONASOL authorities initiated development programs in regions where the PRI lost badly to the PRD in 1988: the Plan Michoacán was established in January 1989, and the Plan Nueva Laguna six months later. Further, states where the PRI had suffered electoral setbacks in 1988 ranked among those receiving the largest amounts of PRONASOL funds in 1989 (Valdez 1990: 13). In Morelos, where Salinas lagged behind Cárdenas by over 70,000 votes, federal investment, in the form of PRONASOL funds, increased by 50 percent (*Proceso* 1990a).

México State has become a showcase for PRONASOL social strategies and political accomplishments. The region was the site of an electoral catastrophe for Carlos Salinas and the PRI in July 1988. By official results, Salinas obtained only 26.7 percent of the vote, in contrast to the 50.4 percent garnered by Cuauhtémoc Cárdenas and the 21.1 percent drawn by Manuel Clouthier of the PAN, and the official party lost in 80 out of 121 municipalities. Since then federal, state, and municipal authorities have channeled an unspecified amount of funds into public works, including installing electricity and building the Xico Solidarity Urban Center in the Chalco Valley, one of the state's poorest areas. Salinas demonstrated his personal interest in Chalco when he spent a highly publicized stay at the home of a local family. Then, during a 1990 tour, he announced the creation of the Chalco 2000 project, designed to provide electricity and water, and he later invited the pope to view what had been accomplished.

During the 1991 local elections in México State, the electoral intentions of PRONASOL were revealed in a memorandum forwarded by Salinas to the governor, Ignacio Pichardo Pagaza, suggesting that the PRI stress PRONASOL's accomplishments in the area. During the electoral campaign, Salinas toured the state, distributing land titles and inaugurating public works. Days before the elections in Chalco, PRI militants distributed basic foodstuffs carrying PRONASOL labels.[12] In contrast with its dismal performance in 1988, in 1991 the PRI won an overwhelming although highly disputed victory, chalking up 121 out of 123 municipalities, including Chalco (Dresser 1990), and totaling 11,852 votes,

---

[12]Interview with Adriana Díaz Barriga, state coordinator of the PAN's organizational office, Mexico City, November 14, 1990.

compared to the PRD total of 2,384 (Secretaría de Acción Electoral n.d.).

PRONASOL's impact on voting behavior is difficult to gauge, given that the study of electoral patterns and public opinion is relatively new in Mexico. What is evident, however, is that PRO-NASOL — along with other instruments such as electoral laws and institutions—enhances the PRI's competitive stance vis-à-vis other parties by undertaking speedy public works projects, delivering goods, and buying clienteles. PRONASOL has clearly influenced the PRI's strong showing in recent electoral contests. In July 1991 the PRI's gubernatorial candidate in Nuevo León won more than 60 percent of the vote in an election that even opposition leaders acknowledged was unusually free of fraud. Prior to the election, Nuevo León received a slew of federally funded public works projects, including "Solidarity," an international bridge to Texas. In a similar vein, two weeks before the midterm elections of August 1991, Salinas toured Mexico and personally handed out in less than ten days as many land titles as distributed by the Mexican government over the past fourteen years (*El Financiero* 1991).

A Mexican political analyst observed after the November 1990 elections in México State that the people were not voting anti-PRI in 1988; they were voting to get the old PRI back, the PRI that was good to them (personal interview, Mexico City, November 11, 1990). PRONASOL's impact on popular movements and electoral outcomes since then seems to be the proof of the pudding. An overall drop in support for the PRD hints that PRONASOL has successfully addressed the grievances of those groups that previously welcomed the PRI in its role as guarantor of material benefits, and manifested their displeasure over the loss of those benefits by voting for the opposition in 1988. The Salinas government gambled on reincorporating large sectors of the population under its mantle through concertation strategies and the provision of public services. Salinas wagered that insofar as popular groups participated in solving community problems and became beneficiaries of development projects, they would lose their incentive to vote for the opposition and either support the PRI or abstain. The gamble paid off: in the 1991 midterm election the PRI scored a landslide, recovering most of the ground lost to the opposition two and a half years earlier.

A Post-PRI Substitute or a Refurbished PRI?

The reemergence of clientelist ties through PRONASOL has important implications for the PRI. One effect of the economic crisis on the ruling party was the erosion of its credibility among the bottom rungs of its corporatist structure. As wages decreased and living standards fell, the PRI began to experience a crisis of representation. The PRI's intricate network of patron-client relations acted as a filter against demands from the base levels of the working-class and campesino sectors, whose members began to feel that their interests were no longer adequately represented.

If the 1930s were the period of corporatist construction, the 1980s were the period of corporatist dismantling. With the outbreak of the debt crisis, popular movements and disaffected groups affiliated to the PRI began to challenge the traditional forms of political and economic control. In their struggle to obtain representation, these groups rejected the clientelist patterns of control in general and the exclusionary policies of the PRI in particular (see Foweraker 1990). Popular movements constantly seek linkage in order to solve immediate problems and satisfy concrete demands. In a context marked by economic decline and the unraveling of the social pact, clientelism and corporatism denied linkage and prevented effective representation. In response, popular movements established alliances built around horizontal networks of leadership and solidarity, which rendered the use of traditional forms of PRI control increasingly ineffective. The Mexico City earthquakes in 1985 provided a dramatic illustration. Alternative projects proposed by popular movements forced the government to abandon or modify its own renewal projects in the face of popular mobilization and organization. This successful challenge to the clientelistic assumptions of the government led to the formation of neighborhood committees, the election of representatives to the Federal District Assembly, the demand for an elective government in Mexico City, and a land-slide electoral victory for the opposition throughout the capital in July 1988.

Events in Mexico City illustrated a nationwide trend: the PRI faltered in the 1980s because it could not respond to popular demands for participation and also because it failed to provide the usual material rewards. PRONASOL represents an effort to recon-struct party-society linkages on both these fronts: it combines refurbished clientelism with fostering popular participation through the promotion of social welfare. PRONASOL's institu-tions, such as the solidarity committees, are serving the govern-ment as a parallel channel for liaison between state and society in a context of weakening corporatism and a declining PRI.

Through their emphasis on concertation, participatory frame-works (like the provision of manual labor), and community-based leadership, PRONASOL programs create a sense of inclusion and serve as agencies through which popular groups can express their demands. If the PRI withers away, the networks established by PRONASOL, through its 50,000 solidarity committees, might serve as new vehicles for representation and control. In PRO-NASOL, government elites may be constructing a more concerted and a more centralized form of political mediation, capable of providing a post-PRI substitute.

PRONASOL's selective support of pro-Salinas factions within the PRI could provide clientelistic rule based on exchanging favors for votes and/or exercising control over popular groups. To the extent that the PRI benefits from PRONASOL and its electoral impact, the program might be able to prevent further party de-cline. As Francisco Escobedo, former PRI undersecretary for social action, recognized: "If the *priístas* take over PRONASOL, it will mean the emergence of a new party, a different party that will have regained the ability to organize social groups. PRONASOL is the PRI under a different name" (personal interview, Mexico City, September 5, 1990). The PRI is already grooming community program leaders for local politics (*New York Times* 1991). If the PRI recovers thanks to PRONASOL, so much the better. If it does not, Salinas or his successor might have in PRONASOL a backup organization and a constituency to go along with it.

It is unclear to what extent PRONASOL's clientelist strategies will be able to rebuild a long-term electoral base for the ruling party. Most analysts believe that the PRI's electoral rebound in August 1991 was largely a reflection of Salinas's personal popu-larity. Electoral campaigns strove to identify Salinas with PRO-NASOL and then link both to the PRI candidates. Votes for the PRI were votes for Salinas and an endorsement of his policies rather than support for the party per se. As a critic of PRONASOL observed:

> Votes don't come out of the PRI machinery any-
> more. They are manufactured by PRONASOL,
> and they are labeled votes for the PRI only for
> purposes of political marketing. But they are
> PRONASOL-Salinas votes (Aguilar Zínser 1991).

Relying on PRONASOL and Salinas as vote-catchers has translated into support for the PRI in a nationwide election. The question
is whether that support can be institutionalized beyond Salinas's
term, and whether the 1994 presidential candidate will be willing
to govern in tandem with PRONASOL. If the past is any indication,
PRONASOL will end—like its predecessors—with the change in
administration. Alternately, the incoming president might transform a refurbished PRI into the "Party of Solidarity."

Meanwhile, the PRI still plays a central role in articulating
political ideals and channeling political participation for certain
sectors, and the institutional ties PRONASOL is contributing are
still tenuous and diffuse. Given this state of affairs, Salinas may
opt to continue governing with the PRI, for lack of a better
alternative, or use PRONASOL to spur the PRI's internal reform
process. PRONASOL's new alliance with popular movements
could be used to force the party to improve its leadership, organization, accountability, responsiveness to the electorate, and electoral performance—or face replacement.

The case of the CDP in Durango is particularly illustrative of
how the government uses its support for new forms of political
representation as a means of pressuring the PRI. After breaking
with the PRD, the CDP initiated a political process which culmi-
nated with the registration of its own political party. The CDP
party did well, becoming the third most powerful electoral force in
Durango, behind the PRI and the faltering PAN, and giving rise to
accusations of veiled financial assistance from the Salinas administration. The case underscores Salinas's interest in promoting a new
set of political leaders to replace inefficient and often corrupt
regional bosses. By recognizing these new intermediaries, the
government is also challenging the local PRI to modernize and
democratize.

Under mounting pressure from the government, PRI officials
have struggled to redefine the PRI's future course in PRONASOL
terms. The "modernizing" wing of the PRI, led by Luis Donaldo
Colosio, now refers to the party as the Party of Solidarity, and in
May 1990 the PRI's National Executive Council announced the

party's Program of Social Solidarity, designed to mobilize and organize citizens around social demands. Internal PRI documents also reveal an increasing emphasis on the connections between the program and the party's stance:

> The president's National Solidarity Program offers us the possibility of promoting small public works that address major concerns. From basic demands we can generate political action plans for the neighborhood, the community, and the municipality . . . thus strengthening the social and electoral perspectives of our party. PRONASOL can be a great instrument for the consolidation of our party (Alfaro Cáceres [former regional secretary of the PRI's National Executive Council] n.d.).

In November 1990, Ignacio Ovalle, head of CONASUPO and coordinator of the *tortivale* program, was named the PRI's secretary for social action.[13] Ovalle's experience in poverty alleviation programs has helped the PRI tie into PRONASOL strategies, such as the selective distribution of coupons—with PRI and PRONASOL logos intertwined—to groups that demonstrate their loyalty to the ruling party. As Ovalle explicitly stated:

> The PRI will demand that PRONASOL provide support to our members. And if other people organize themselves, let them receive [the program's] benefits too, but not at the expense of the organization that good *priístas* have already achieved (*El Sol de México*, March 1, 1991).

PRONASOL delegates frequently pressure urban and rural popular organizations to join forces with the PRI or be excluded from the program's benefits. For example, *tortivale* coupons were not distributed in forty-eight neighborhoods in Mexico City where mobilization by non-*priísta* popular organizations and by PRD supporters—like the Asamblea de Barrios and the Alianza Vecinal—had been significant. Another example was the exclusion of several organizations linked to the independent National Coordinating Committee of Coffee Producing Organizations (CNOC) from concertation agreements because they were reluctant to en-

---

[13]Ovalle had previously occupied two other posts in poverty-related programs. Under López Portillo he was head of the National Indigenous Institute (INI) and also coordinator of the National Plan for Economically Depressed Zones and Marginal Groups (COPLAMAR).

gage in PRI politics. In San Luis Potosí, where the Frente Cívico Popular, a coalition of opposition groups, won the municipal presidency, municipal authorities lament the lack of PRONASOL resources to carry out public works, and charge that the federal government is withholding resources in order to undermine the credibility and image of opposition municipal president Guillermo Pizzuto. In the state of Hidalgo, the federal government and the regional delegation of the Ministry of Budget and Planning have refused PRONASOL benefits to social groups organized outside of the official party (Moguel 1990). PRD municipal authorities throughout the country have accused the PRI of hoarding PRONASOL resources instead of delivering them to local governments (*La Jornada* 1990). PRONASOL highlights the costs of allying with the opposition, and by so doing it may eventually help coax the electorate back into the PRI fold.

The program may also be strengthening the PRI as PRONASOL resources are used to target flows to key regions, especially before elections. As one very influential political commentator argued, the electoral connection between PRONASOL and the PRI is clearly established:

> The political current represented by PRONASOL will be a determining factor in the 1991 elections. In itself, PRONASOL has become a parallel PRI; its delegates are the new political class of *salinismo*; they arrive with power and money. . . . As long as it lasts—not beyond the *sexenio*—PRONASOL will be the new instrument of control of the current government. Many will enter politics as representatives of the Party of Solidarity. The presence of this program will be key, because it will invest money in opposition areas to regain the vote for the PRI. That's why the voice of Solidarity within the system at the hour of deciding candidates will be fundamental (Ramírez 1991).

PRONASOL has altered PRI practices—such as candidate selection—and even its ideology to reflect the economic, political, and social orientations mapped out by the *salinista* elite. PRONASOL regional coordinators figured prominently as PRI candidates to the Senate and Chamber of Deputies for the 1991 midterm elections (and they won by larger margins than other *priístas*). And while the PRI once spoke in terms of classes and social justice, PRONASOL forms alliances with groups outside the party's corporatist structure and speaks of co-participation.

However, these transformations do not indicate a structural break with traditional forms of government response to political upheavals. In the aftermath of the 1968 student revolt, President Luis Echeverría—trying to shore up the government's credibility—established ties with disaffected groups outside of the PRI, incorporated new faces into the political elite, and instituted a new ideological framework based on the notion of "shared development." The similarities in style and objectives between PRONASOL and the co-optation strategies employed by previous administrations suggest that PRONASOL is less innovative than its apostles have claimed. It may simply be a reenactment of a familiar pattern, whereby the government pours resources into areas where the opposition has sprung up, restructures the ruling party, establishes renewed clientelistic ties, and ultimately returns to some form of politics as usual.

PRONASOL has not led to greater decentralization of power, but rather to reinvigorated presidentialism. Salinas came into office on the coattails of a weakened and ineffectual predecessor; his image was further tainted by claims of electoral fraud. Shortly after his inauguration, Salinas devised a personal style of governance which combines preemptive strikes, dramatic actions, and the selective use of force to impress the public and transmit an implicit message: "There is a government; there is a president." PRONASOL, as an essential vehicle for the display of symbolic politics, has assisted Salinas in the crucial task of strengthening the presidency. A key component of the program is the active presidential presence in the countryside. Salinas leaves the official residence on a weekly whirlwind tour to fulfill old commitments to popular groups and make new ones. Salinas's personal presence, commitment, and activism build upon the *caudillista* strains in Mexico's political culture and enhance the president's stature among those sectors of the population that support authoritative leadership. When Salinas toured the Laguna region as a presidential candidate in 1988, he was received with threats, recriminations, and anger. Two years and many PRONASOL projects later, Salinas was greeted as a national hero.

PRONASOL also strengthens Salinas insofar as its resources are used in a clientelistic fashion to allocate rewards and punishments to local power groups in a political system where all financial roads begin at Los Pinos, the presidential residence. PRONASOL's political machine operates in a personalistic fashion, and local elites and community leaders compete for access to state funds for their own clienteles. Those who have gained entry to the Salinas coterie usually obtain funds; those who have not usually do not. Through PRONASOL Salinas is altering the regional power balance in his favor, by displacing foes—such as governors ambivalent about "modernization"—and replacing them with PRO-NASOL delegates, labeled "the new political class of salinismo."[14]

Concentrating public funds for development projects in PRO-NASOL enables the Salinas team not only to divert funds from the opposition but also to short-circuit traditional allocations of PRI patronage. Many PRONASOL projects are the sort that in the past were handled by PRI politicians in local, state, and federal government. Now those politicians must negotiate with PRONASOL delegates, Salinas's personal representatives in the countryside, in order to receive financing for projects for their areas. PRONASOL coordinators hold responsibilities that were previously in the hands of municipal presidents and state governors, such as disbursing funds and selecting development undertakings. In December 1989 in the state of México, for example, the funds that local deputies formerly could use for public works were suspended and rechanneled to PRONASOL and its regional delegates (*Proceso* 1990b). PRONASOL coordinators have been nicknamed "vicegovernors" in recognition of their power over resources and the political loyalties this creates. Rogelio Montemayor and Manuel Cavazos Lerma, two PRONASOL coordinators (and recently elected PRI senators) in Coahuila and Tamaulipas, respectively, are well-known Salinas allies and declared supporters of the restructuring program. In their previous posts as presidents of planning and budget committees within the Chamber of Deputies, they supervised PRONASOL funds.

As PRONASOL has displaced traditional sources of patronage, it has engendered divisiveness and disruption among Mexico's political elite. Because of its implications for the balance of power between Mexico City and the state capitals, several governors have opposed PRONASOL and its arbitrary channeling of funds through its regional representatives. In Oaxaca, for example, tensions between the federal and state governments were exacerbated by publicized disputes between the PRONASOL delegate and Oaxaca's governor, Heladio Ramírez, about resource allocation and the timely completion of public works. In the case of PRONASOL negotiations with the CDP in Durango, Salinas strained relations with important state and party actors opposed to political reform, particularly Governor José Ramírez Gamero. Ramírez

[14]The removal of governors perceived as dysfunctional (corrupt or incapable of guaranteeing electoral victories for the PRI) has become a trademark of the Salinas style of governance. In his first two years in office, Salinas removed four governors: Luis Martínez Villicaña from Michoacán, Xicotencatl Leyva from Baja California Norte, Mario Ramón Beteta from the state of México, and Víctor Manzanilla Schaffer from Yucatán.

Gamero—who in the 1988 presidential race came out early and strong in favor of Alfredo del Mazo—recently launched a virulent attack on PRONASOL, declaring that program funds were not adequately channeled and that it was very difficult to establish solidarity committees (*Proceso* 1990a: 12). In another highly publicized display of presidential power, Salinas forced the governor of Nayarit to purge his cabinet due to alleged misappropriation of PRONASOL funds in his state (*Christian Science Monitor* 1991). These cases illustrate the kinds of pressures that affect local forms of representation and federal officials as PRONASOL saturates the country's institutional terrain with its own representatives. Many PRI leaders resent the fact that PRONASOL circumvents their authority and establishes rivals—in the form of PRONASOL delegates—in their areas of responsibility.

PRONASOL's selective displacement of traditional forms of mediation and leadership has also opened a political void that members of the upper ranks of the executive branch have increasingly begun to fill (Schmidt 1990). The new strategy of the Salinas government toward social movements and popular groups is to negotiate broadly and try to reach agreements. The objective is to establish a direct dialogue between the president and his cabinet and these groups and to eliminate the bureaucracy that hinders the negotiating task. Thus, the concertation strategies espoused by PRONASOL represent a convergence of the interests of many popular organizations, as well as those of the technocratic-modernizing sectors within the PRI and the government. The appointment of PRONASOL technobureaucrats to posts previously occupied by longtime politicos, however, may not mean a fundamental restructuring of power relations that would lead to more accountable and representative leaders. Instead, it may merely be a replacement of traditional power holders with new elites loyal to the Salinas administration.

As Fox and Gordillo (1989) have argued, traditional elites are often replaced by new concentrations of power, modernizing rather than eliminating *caciquismo*. The discretionary control that the Salinas team of technobureaucrats exercises over PRONASOL enables it to undermine the network of bureaucratic and corrupt practices associated with the "old" PRI. But in reality, many local and regional political elites who were supposedly to be bypassed by the program are its prime beneficiaries. In many regions of Mexico, municipal authorities refuse PRONASOL funds to groups not affiliated to the PRI, or they reward political loyalty by overlooking the co-participation provision. The "direct and transparent" distribution of resources oftentimes is sabotaged by municipal authorities who have mastered the art of channeling public resources into private pockets. In other cases, PRONASOL contracts for public works go to individuals or companies with insufficient technical capabilities but with close ties to high-ranking municipal officials from the PRI. PRONASOL emphasizes identifying "natural leaders" in popular communities, but frequently those leaders turn out to be *priístas* of the old-guard variety who use their influence to create solidarity committees that mirror the regional powers that be. Salinas used PRONASOL to rid himself of some unwanted allies, but the survival of many traditional PRI structures and practices seems to indicate that Salinas is still willing to bet his political future on the ruling party.

Unlikely Partners:
PRONASOL and Democracy

PRONASOL is evidence of the intertwined political and economic logics upon which Mexico's economic adjustment strategy is based. It is a strategy which couples major attempts to increase economic efficiency and reduce state intervention with substantial amounts of politically motivated, often inefficient disbursements such as the funds channeled through PRONASOL. The objective of this two-pronged strategy is to assure political consensus and create conditions for further economic liberalization. Under the rubric of modernization, government elites are engineering a transition from ubiquitous state intervention in the economy to strategic, targeted, and compensatory intervention in the social welfare sphere. Thus the Salinas regime is using PRONASOL to accomplish both political and economic goals, sending out an explicit message justifying further economic liberalization while simultaneously emphasizing the state's commitment to popular groups. Just like its predecessors (CONASUPO and COPLAMAR), PRONASOL's political purpose is to appear to further social justice, and thereby legitimate the regime.

Preliminary assessments of PRONASOL indicate that the economic measures enacted through its programs rarely represent a resource transfer that is long term and income producing for the avowed beneficiaries. When judged in terms of its economic effects, PRONASOL appears as a program with limited redistributive impact, designed to provide selective compensations to populations which cannot be incorporated into the formal economy. PRONASOL undoubtedly mitigates some of the harm done by economic depression, but it does not address the structural causes of poverty. A frontal attack on poverty would entail macroeconomic policies focused on generating employment and elevating income. The current direction of Mexico's political economy, however, indicates that public choice increasingly favors efficiency at the expense of redistribution. Social spending through PRONASOL is commendable, but PRONASOL alone cannot neutralize the effects of a restructuring program that further skews the country's income distribution.

PRONASOL's limited capacity to alleviate poverty may also result from the program's increasing politicization. By responding to political imperatives, the program has targeted groups that do not classify as the very poor, placed a disproportionate priority on providing benefits to the urban poor, and expanded geographically and financially for reasons that go beyond poverty alleviation. While PRONASOL may be contributing to a minimal safety net for the lowest-income population through social selectivity in subsidy delivery, this delivery is not free of political strings.

PRONASOL forms part of a broader political dynamic, namely, the creation of alliances between public and popular organizations as a way of diffusing the latters' political struggles. PRONASOL is reorienting the content of popular demands toward social issues, and then channeling them into state-sponsored institutional arrangements that deliver material rewards. As such, PRONASOL marks the emergence of a renewed and rationalized clientelism based on not-so-new forms of consultation and concertation between the state and civil society. The fact that clientelism is alive and well suggests that powerful institutional arrangements and routines survived the tidal wave of 1988, and that three years later they are still able to constrain popular forces. The institutional and bureaucratic networks that PRONASOL has contributed may portend a reinforcement of effective state control over the political arena.

PRONASOL does indeed promote linkage between the government and popular groups, but not necessarily democratic linkage. It often reinforces the PRI's standard operating procedures and reproduces familiar patterns of PRI domination. There are no democratic controls over the PRI's spending of PRONASOL funds or over the individuals and organizations that carry out PRONASOL's diverse programs. By channeling PRONASOL's resources into the never-ending network of traditional power structures, the PRI has been able to make popular issues its own once again and to enhance its responsiveness to popular demands, but this increased responsiveness has not been accompanied by reforms that would enforce government accountability.

According to a high-ranking state official, "PRONASOL is evidence that there is a will to promote political liberalization. But the program's contradictions show that there is also a will to remain in power" (personal interview, Mexico City, November 13, 1990). PRONASOL underscores the need to work in concert with popular groups, but the program's institutional arrangements are designed to provide the political elite with a large degree of centralized authority. PRONASOL avowedly respects the autonomy of popular organizations, yet the PRI has conditioned the delivery of resources to political loyalty. Government elites concentrate discretionary powers in their own hands so as to be able to target PRONASOL resources to the very poor, but enhanced discretionary powers may provide fertile ground for increased authoritarianism. Although PRONASOL's stated objectives could be interpreted as an attempt to promote political opening, many of its tactics suggest that government elites are unwilling to surrender political control. PRONASOL has allowed Salinas to reactivate the vast and powerful machinery of renewed presidentialism—which does not augur well for the future of institutionalized politics in Mexico.

Ultimately the degree of representation and popular participation that PRONASOL offers will depend on Mexican leaders' resolve to promote genuine political democratization. Democratization requires open competition for control of government, and this requires free and fair elections. Fair elections, in turn, require a level playing field for all contenders. Yet PRONASOL is rigging the game in favor of the PRI and against opposition parties with limited resources.

While new, direct relationships are being established between the state and popular organizations, electoral democracy and equality of conditions among parties still remain elusive goals. The PRONASOL-PRI alliance has been slow to respond to political demands such as respect for the vote, but it is quick to respond to demands for water, sewerage, electricity, and inclusion in solidarity committees. This responsiveness to social demands may be an attempt to reproduce—at least selectively—the arrangements associated with Mexico's traditional social pact.

This exchange of material resources for political support or nonconfrontation may seem a matter of small concern for those in Mexico who are weary of the political battle, but those groups and individuals who are not quite ready to abandon the democratic ideal have reason to view the emergence of PRONASOL and the weakening of explicitly political demands with some trepidation. The new links PRONASOL is forging between the state and society will not necessarily lead to electoral democracy; if anything, PRONASOL's success may indicate that those who would rule by manipulation have developed greater skill in doing so.

References

Acosta, Carlos, and Gerardo Galarza. 1989. "Los secretarios de Hacienda y Programación prometen un México totalmente distinto al final de 1990," *Proceso*, November 27.

Aguilar Zínser, Adolfo. 1991. "Presidencialismo sin partidos," *El Financiero*, September 9.

Alfaro Cáceres, José Encarnación. n.d. "Solidaridad social y planeación política." Mimeo.

Aziz Nassif, Alberto. 1990. "¿Una reforma solidaria?" *La Jornada*, August 7.

CCPNS (Consejo Consultivo del Programa Nacional de Solidaridad). 1990. *El combate a la pobreza*. Mexico: El Nacional.

Christian Science Monitor. 1991. "Mexican President Wins Plaudits with Aid to the Poor," March 19.

Dresser, Denise. 1990. "Another Turn of the Salinas Screw: November 1990 Elections in the State of México." Paper presented at the Research Seminar on Mexico and U.S.-Mexican Relations, University of California, San Diego, November. Mimeo.

———. n.d. "Of Friends and Foes: Economic Liberalization and Political Coalitions in Mexico." Ph.D. dissertation, Princeton University, forthcoming.

El Financiero (Mexico City). 1991. "Elecciones de medio sexenio: Solidaridad con el PRI," *El Financiero Informe Especial* 2:70 (September 13).

El Nacional (Mexico City). 1991. "Solidaridad en 1991," Suplemento Gaceta Solidaria, March 4.

Foweraker, Joe. 1990. "Popular Movements and Political Change in Mexico." In *Popular Movements and Political Change in Mexico*, edited by Joe Foweraker and Ann L. Craig. Boulder, Colo.: Lynne Rienner, in association with the Center for U.S.-Mexican Studies, University of California, San Diego.

Fox, Jonathan. 1986. "The Political Dynamics of Reform: The Case of the Mexican Food System, 1980–1982." Ph.D. dissertation, Massachusetts Institute of Technology.

————. 1991. "Popular Participation and Access to Food: Mexico's Community Food Councils, 1979–1986." In *Food Security and Hunger in Central America and Mexico*, edited by Scott Whiteford and Ann Ferguson. Boulder, Colo.: Westview.

Fox, Jonathan, and Gustavo Gordillo. 1989. "Between State and Market: The Campesinos' Quest for Autonomy." In *Mexico's Political Futures*, edited by Wayne A. Cornelius, Judith Gentleman, and Peter H. Smith. Monograph Series, no. 30. La Jolla: Center for U.S.-Mexican Studies, University of California, San Diego.

García Soler, León. 1989. "Acuerdo democrático más allá del debate político: entrevista con Carlos Salinas de Gortari," *Jueves de Excélsior* 3503 (September 7).

GEA (Grupo de Economistas y Asociados). 1991. *GEA Económico*, April.

Haber, Paul L. 1989. "Cárdenas, Salinas, and Urban Popular Movements in Mexico: The Case of the CDP in Durango." Paper presented at the Latin American Studies Association Fifteenth Annual Meeting, Miami, Florida, December 4–6.

Harvey, Neil. 1990. "The Limits of Concertation in Rural Mexico, 1988–1990." Paper presented to the research workshop "Mexico in Transition: Elements of Continuity and Change," Institute of Latin American Studies, London, May 18–19.

IMF (International Monetary Fund). 1991. *Government Finance Statistics Yearbook, 1990.* Ann Arbor, Mich.: IMF.

La Jornada (Mexico City). 1990. "Se desvían fondos del PRONASOL en Michoacán, denunció el PRD," September 26.

Levy, Santiago. 1991. "Poverty Alleviation in Mexico." Mimeo.

Loaeza, Soledad. 1989. "El regreso del Estado: por un nuevo intervencionismo," *Cuadernos de Nexos* 17 (November).

Macías García, Javier. 1991. "Compromiso en marcha: entrevista con Olga Elena Peña Martínez, Jefa de la Unidad de Atención a la Ciudadanía," *El Nacional*, special supplement, February 8.

Moguel, Julio. 1990. "National Solidarity Program Fails to Help the Very Poor," *Voices of Mexico* (Universidad Nacional Autónoma de México) 15 (October–December).

————. 1991. "Local Power and Development Alternatives: The Experience of the Urban Popular Movement in a Region of Northern Mexico." Paper presented at the Latin American Studies Association Sixteenth Annual Meeting, Washington, D.C., April 4–6.

New York Times. 1991. "Mexicans Reinvent the Pork Barrel," August 16.

Presidencia de la República Mexicana. n.d. *Solidaridad en México*. Mexico: Presidencia.

Proceso. 1990a. "El PRONASOL, medio de liquidación del federalismo," October 29.

————. 1990b. "Recursos, obras, leyes, todo para que el PRI recupere votos en el estado de México," March 26.

Provencio, Enrique. 1990. "Solidaridad: alcances y límites," *La Jornada*, August 3.

Ramírez, Carlos. 1991. "Indicador político," *El Financiero*, March 19.

Rascón, Marco. 1990. "Solidaridad: sentimiento noble," *La Jornada*, August 7.

Rojas, Carlos. 1990. "El Programa Nacional de Solidaridad: responsabilidad social y compromiso de gobierno." Address to the Congreso Binacional on "El primer año de gobierno del Licenciado Carlos Salinas de Gortari," Austin, Texas, February 22.

Salinas de Gortari, Carlos. 1984. "Production and Participation in Rural Areas: Some Political Considerations." In *The Political Economy of Income Distribution in Mexico*, edited by Pedro Aspe and Javier Beristain. New York: Holmes and Meier.

————. 1988. Address establishing the Comisión Nacional de Programas de Solidaridad Social, reprinted in *Textos básicos sobre el Programa Nacional de Solidaridad*. Mexico.

Schmidt, Samuel. 1990. "Redefinición de liderazgos," *Examen* 15 (August 15).

Secretaría de Acción Nacional. n.d. "Resultados electorales por municipio y partido en 1981, 1984, 1987 y 1990." Mexico: Secretaría de Acción Nacional, Partido Revolucionario Institucional.

Sheahan, John. 1991. *Conflict and Change in Mexican Economic Strategy: Implications for Mexico and for Latin America*. Monograph Series, no. 34. La Jolla: Center for U.S.-Mexican Studies, University of California, San Diego.

Solís Cámara, Fernando. 1991. "El combate a la pobreza: una opción a la democracia," *Examen* 2:2 (September).

Valdez, Guillermo. 1990. "Evaluación del Programa Nacional de Solidaridad," *Examen* 12 (May).

Acronyms

CDP	Comité de Defensa Popular/Committee for Popular Defense
CIOAC	Central Independiente de Obreros Agrícolas y Campesinos/Independent Confederation of Agricultural Workers and Peasants
CNOC	Coordinadora Nacional de Organizaciones Cafetaleras/National Coordinating Committee of Coffee-Producing Organizations
CNPA	Coordinadora Nacional "Plan de Ayala"/National "Plan de Ayala" Coordinating Committee
CONAMUP	Coordinadora Nacional del Movimiento Urbano Popular/National Coordinating Committee of the Urban Popular Movement
CONASUPO	Compañía Nacional de Subsistencias Populares/National Staple Products Company
COPLAMAR	Coordinación General del Plan Nacional de Zonas Deprimidas y Grupos Marginados/National Plan for Economically Depressed Regions and Marginalized Groups
DIF	Desarrollo Integral de la Familia/National System for the Integral Development of the Family
FDN	Frente Democrático Nacional/National Democratic Front
FIOAC	Federación Independiente de Obreros Agrícolas y Campesinos/Independent Federation of Agricultural Workers and Peasants
INI	Instituto Nacional Indigenista/National Indigenous Institute
PAN	Partido de Acción Nacional/National Action Party

PECE	Pacto para la Estabilidad y el Crecimiento Económico/Pact for Stability and Economic Growth
PRD	Partido de la Revolución Democrática/Party of the Democratic Revolution
PRI	Partido Revolucionario Institucional/Institutional Revolutionary Party
PRONASOL	Programa Nacional de Solidaridad/National Solidarity Program
PT	Partido del Trabajo/Labor Party
UNORCA	Unión Nacional de Organizaciones Regionales Campesinas/National Union of Regional Peasant Organizations

Denise Dresser is a Ph.D. candidate in the Politics Department at Princeton University and a member of GEA Grupo de Economistas y Asociados, a private consulting firm based in Mexico City. She also teaches at the Instituto Tecnológico Autónomo de México (ITAM).